SCHOLASTIC

Follow-the-Directions
Art Activities

By Teresa Cornell and Amy Weaver

D1609230

NEW YORK • TORONTO • LONDON • AUCKLAND • SYDNEY
MEXICO CITY • NEW DELHI • HONG KONG • BUENOS AIRES

Teaching
Resources

For Frank, Gracie, and Lily:
Here's to all of our love, laughter, and happiness. Love you!
—A.W.

To all the staff, students, and families at Cedar Grove:
Thanks for making teaching fun and exciting!
—T.C.

Acknowledgments

Special thanks to Jeanne Hess, Patti Hughes, Karen Stevenson,
and Terri Schwartz for all of their help and great ideas!

Cover and interior art by James Graham Hale

Cover design by Jason Robinson

Interior design by Sydney Wright

ISBN: 0-439-44990-1
Copyright © 2005 by Teresa Cornell and Amy Weaver
Published by Scholastic Inc.
All rights reserved.
Printed in the U.S.A.

6 7 8 9 10   40   13 12 11 10 09 08

Contents

Introduction

The ability to follow directions is one of the most important skills children must learn in order to succeed in school and throughout their lives. The ability to critically read and understand directions on tests, complete class assignments and homework, fill out forms, and follow the steps of a recipe are just some of the many skills children will be asked to perform in school and throughout their lives.

Following directions accurately has another important benefit—helping children to become independent learners. As they develop this skill and better understand what is expected of them, students become more confident. This confidence sets the stage for them to proceed on their own and take on more complex tasks as they progress through school.

Meeting the Standards

Following written directions is also a critical reading skill. According to Mid-continent Research for Education and Learning (McRel), a nationally recognized nonprofit organization that collects and synthesizes national and state K–12 standards, students in grades K–2 should be able to use reading skills and strategies to understand and interpret a variety of informational texts, including written directions.

The reading and language arts curriculum for the Maryland school district in which we teach states: "Reading to perform a task is a complex process that requires not only an understanding of informational text, including its structure and organization, but also the ability to act upon the comprehension." This process includes opportunities for students to read and comprehend directions in order to follow the steps to complete a task, such as following a recipe, conducting a science experiment, following directions to play a game, or creating an art project.

Each of the 20 simple, easy-to-make art activities in this book gives children the opportunity to practice reading and following directions to perform a task. Because they connect to seasonal and holiday themes, you can use these activities all year long. Each project includes a reproducible mini-poster (see page 6) with step-by-step directions for students to follow; a list of needed materials, tools, and patterns; tips for making the project go smoothly, warm-up and extension activities; as well as literature links that relate to the project's theme.

Strategies for Student Success

The ability to read and follow directions to perform a task requires students to apply strategies before, during, and after reading. Following are suggestions and strategies to review with students before they start on

Source: *Content Knowledge: A Compendium of Standards and Benchmarks for K–12 Education*, 4th Edition (Mid-Continent Research for Education and Learning, 2003)

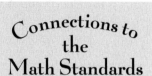

Connections to the Math Standards

The activities in this book also provide opportunities for students to build several mathematical skills and concepts, including:

* number sense
* one-to-one correspondence
* counting
* ordinal numbers
* directionality (top, bottom, middle, right, left, on the back, up, down, upside-down)
* fractions
* geometry (shapes, points, corners)
* size (large, small, long, short)
* patterns

the projects. For an example of a teacher-student dialogue that models how to introduce the activities, refer to page 7.

Students must first establish a purpose for reading; they must be prepared to read the directions in order to complete the task. Discuss with students why they will be reading these directions, focusing on the importance of reading to perform a task. Relate the activity students are going to do to previous classroom experiences they have had, such as playing learning games or science experiments, if you have included these in your program. Also encourage students to think of experiences outside the classroom that require reading directions. They may recollect experiences at home such as cooking with a family member, preparing to take a trip to a new place, or making another craft or art project.

Before they begin, students must look at the materials list and a sample of the completed product, and check to see if they have all the necessary supplies. Talk with them about the materials they will need to complete the activity. Show them the patterns, the pieces of precut construction paper, and other necessary materials and tools that each craft may require.

Students must read through the directions to see what types of actions they will take in order to complete the activity. Help them focus on the key action words used in each step, such as *trace*, *cut*, *fold*, *draw*, *glue*, and so on. Encourage students to predict which supplies might be needed as suggested by these action words, such as pencils, scissors, crayons, and glue. Also review and demonstrate directional words such as *next to*, *under*, and below.

To complete the task, students must read the directions step by step, performing the actions as instructed. The directions in each activity are written in sequential order, so it is important that students are familiar with ordinal numbers. Point out the ordinal numbers at the beginning of each step, and discuss their meaning and the necessity of completing each step in order. Ask students to share their thoughts about why they must follow the steps in order, and what might happen if they do not follow the sequence. Have students read one direction at a time and think about it until they understand exactly what they are being asked to do. You might suggest that they check off each step as they complete it.

Students must look for clues to help them decode the text. The activities are written in simple, primary language and include rebus-style picture clues, numerals, and highlighted words to aid students in the process. Included with each step is an illustration of how the product looks at that stage. This will help students check that they are following the directions correctly. As you walk students through each step, model for them how to read the directions using the picture clues. During this

Tips for Success

❁ Post a list of materials needed for the activity next to the directions so that students can check independently to see if they are ready to begin.

❁ To make the patterns sturdier, cut them out of tagboard and label each one. Consider making additional sets of patterns so there are enough for more than one student to use at a time.

❁ We have found that as our students became more independent, it was better to omit having a sample finished product available for them to see. This ensured that they actually read the directions, rather than simply mimicking the sample when creating their own.

❁ Encourage students to add their own personal touches to their projects.

TIP

On the inside back cover of this book, you'll find a set of ready-to-reproduce pictures and labels that you can use to create directions for other art activities your students can undertake.

Extending Learning

❋ **Create a Craft** Invite children to come up with their own easy art projects and create step-by-step directions for their classmates to follow.

❋ **"Paper Plate" Comes Before "Pipe Cleaner"** Ask students to alphabetize the materials and tools needed to complete each project.

❋ **Scrambled Steps** Cut the steps on a mini-poster into strips. Then scramble them and place in a pocket chart. Challenge students to put the steps in the correct order.

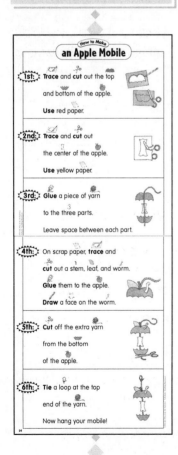

first experience, you may want to create the craft with students to show them how the project will look after each step.

After completing the activity, students should go back over the steps to make sure they have followed the directions correctly and haven't skipped any steps. Model for students how to go back and review the directions, checking that they have completed all of the steps. Encourage them to ask themselves questions such as, "Have I completed every step?" and "Did I follow the directions correctly?"

Setting Up Centers

In our classrooms, we often use these activities as literacy centers during our reading block. The center setup allows students to have an opportunity to read independently while also engaging in a fun and enjoyable activity that builds other important skills. Young children need numerous experiences that require cutting, tracing, gluing, and so on, to continue to develop their fine motor skills.

In a center, we place the materials and tools needed for the projects, such as precut paper, glue, patterns, and scissors. We also post a copy of the directions so that one or two students at a time can easily read them. At the beginning of the week, we introduce the center and highlight any text that may be unfamiliar to students or steps that may be challenging. As students become more proficient in following directions and reading to perform a task, they will need less and less support.

Making the Mini-Posters

- To assemble each of the mini-posters that show the step-by-step directions for students to follow, simply photocopy the two (sometimes three) pages of the poster. Cut off the bottom of the first page, and glue or tape it to the top of the second page, as indicated. (Enlarge the pages, if desired.)

- When using the activities with small groups or individuals, you may want to make a copy of the directions for each student. Then students may take home the directions to share with family members and explain how they followed the directions to complete the activity. Students may also wish to do the activity again at home.

- To aid beginning readers, trace or highlight any color words in the corresponding color, turning words into graphic cues. You might also color some of the picture clues to match, for example, the color of construction paper students will be using.

Now you are ready to go! We hope your students enjoy and learn from these Follow-the-Directions Art Activities as much as ours have.

Introducing the Activities: A Student-Teacher Dialogue

The dialogue that follows is a sample teacher-student exchange using the How to Make a Fire Safety Dog Puppet activity. This kind of dialogue can be useful when first embarking on these activities with your class. It suggests possible ways to introduce the activity to students and to talk with them before, during, and after completing the task. An exchange between teacher and students helps students become aware of their purpose for reading as well as learn how to properly read directions in order to complete a task. Once your students have had several experiences with these activities, they will need less support and eventually create the crafts independently.

Teacher: Today we are going to read to perform the task of making a Fire Safety Dog Puppet. We will be reading directions step by step to show how you can make the puppet on your own. Who can think of another time when you have read directions in order to do something or make something?

Student: I remember when we made applesauce and we read the recipe to make it.

Teacher: Good thinking! Can anyone else think of another example, maybe at home?

Student: When I got a new game for my birthday, we read the directions to learn how to play it.

Teacher: That is a great example! Those were both examples of reading to perform a task. (*Display the mini-poster that shows the directions as well as a list of the materials.*) Here are the directions and a list of materials that we will need to make the Fire Safety Dog Puppet. Before we begin, let's take a look at the materials. Who can tell me one thing we will need?

Student: We'll need red and white paper.

Teacher: Yes. We need both red and white construction paper. Is there anything else we will need?

Student: We need a craft stick and a marker.

Teacher: You're exactly right! It's a black marker that we need. We also need the patterns. Now let's look at the directions. What do you notice about how the directions are written?

Student: The directions have a title. I know it's the title because the words are bigger and some of the letters are capitalized.

Teacher: Yes, the title is important because it tells you what you will be making. What else do you see?

Student: The directions have lots of pictures.

Teacher: Why do you think there are pictures in the directions?

Student: I think they are there so you know what to use and you know what to do.

Teacher: Very good. The directions are written with picture clues to show what you need, what to do, and how to do it.

Student: I see numbers.

Teacher: Those numbers are very important when creating this puppet. Why do you think the numbers are there?

Student: I think they tell you all the steps.

Teacher: Excellent! These are ordinal numbers. They are *first*, *second*, *third*, *fourth*, and so on. Each step is numbered so you know when to do it. Why do you think it is necessary to have these numbers?

Student: They are important to show you the order. If we didn't have them, we wouldn't know which step to do first.

Teacher: Exactly. When reading directions, it is very important to do them in order so that you create the project correctly. Looking at some of the other picture clues and words, such as *cut* and *glue*, can you predict any other materials that we will need?

Student: When you cut, you need scissors and when you glue, you need a bottle of glue or a glue stick.

Teacher: Right. We should check to see if we have those materials ready as well. What materials do you think we will need in order to do the third step?

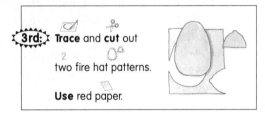

3rd: **Trace** and **cut** out two fire hat patterns. **Use** red paper.

Student: I think we need patterns so we know what to trace and a pencil to trace them with.

Teacher: Good. Let's also check to be sure we have those, too. *(Check with students to be sure all the materials are available.)* Now that we have everything ready, let's read the first step and learn what we do to begin. *(Read the first step aloud.)* In this step, we have learned that we need white paper. Everyone get your piece of white paper ready. Look at the picture to the right of the step.

Who can tell me how we need to fold the paper?

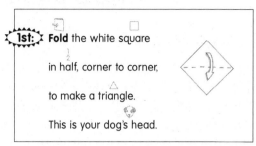

1st: **Fold** the white square in half, corner to corner, to make a triangle. This is your dog's head.

Student: I can tell that we are going to fold the square to make a triangle.

Teacher: Good. Let's try to fold our paper to make it look like the picture. *(Watch to make sure all your students are folding their papers correctly. Remind them to check their paper against the picture provided in the step. Then continue with each step, repeatedly asking questions about the materials, the picture clues, and what the directions say to do. Depending on the reading level and age of your students, you may need to spend more or less time on each step. You also may need to help your students with the reading. Once they have completed the puppet, continue with the dialogue below.)*

Teacher: Now we have completed our Fire Safety Dog Puppet. Let's check back over the directions to make sure we have completed all of the steps. *(Read back over each step, one by one, and have students look at their completed puppets, checking to be sure that they completed each step. You may want to have a sample puppet already created, for which you omitted a step, such as the seventh, in which students are directed to draw a face and spots. Show the puppet to students and ask them what they notice about it. Ask them if the puppet was created by correctly following all the directions.)*

 How to Make

a Shape School Bus

Getting Started

When school starts, big yellow school buses start to roll again. In this activity, students explore familiar shapes as they create a school bus of their own. Begin by talking with children about the attributes of different shapes. For example, a square has four straight sides of the same size, and four corners. A rectangle also has four sides and four corners. However, it has two matching long sides and two matching short sides. Play a game of "I Spy Shapes" and challenge children to look around the classroom for examples of different shapes.

What You Need (for each child)

- Shape School Bus directions, pages 10–11
- school bus patterns, page 24
- yellow construction paper, 9 by 12 inches
- black construction paper, 3 by 6 inches
- white construction paper, 6 by 9 inches
- red construction paper, 4 by 4 inches
- pencil
- scissors
- glue

Tips for Success

❋ Highlight the color words in the directions using markers in corresponding colors.

❋ To make the wheels on the bus actually spin, have students attach them to the bus using paper fasteners.

Do More!

How do children in your class get to school? Do they ride the bus or a train, come by car, or walk? Gather data from children about how they get to school, tally the results, and then create a human graph that shows the way students get to school. Have children stand or sit behind one another in rows. (One row consists of walkers, another bus riders, and so on.) Ask volunteers to draw a picture to represent each group. Then invite students to step out of their row, one by one, and observe the graph (while you take that student's place in the row.) Ask questions, such as, "How do most of the children in our class get to school? How do the fewest children get to school? How many children take the bus?" and so on. Note: If most of your students ride the bus, you might graph which bus numbers they ride.

Literature Links

Axle Annie by Robin Pulver (Puffin Books, 2001) This humorous story tells what happens when Axle Annie, the best school bus driver in town, can't make it up Tiger Hill to get the children to school.

Never Ride Your Elephant to School by Doug Johnson (Henry Holt, 1995) Some kids take the bus, others walk, but the little girl in this zany story rides her elephant to school— with hilarious results!

The Wheels on the Bus by Maryann Kovalski (Little, Brown, 1987) Your students will enjoy this rollicking retelling of an old favorite song.

How to Make
a Shape School Bus

1st:

Trace and **cut** out

 the school bus.

 **Use** yellow paper.

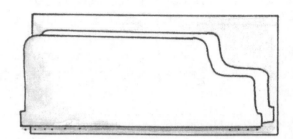

2nd:

Trace and **cut** out

2 two circles.

 **Use** black paper.

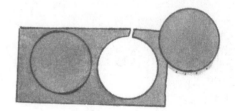

3rd:

For wheels, **glue**

  the circles to the bus.

Follow-the-Directions Art Activities   Scholastic Teaching Resources

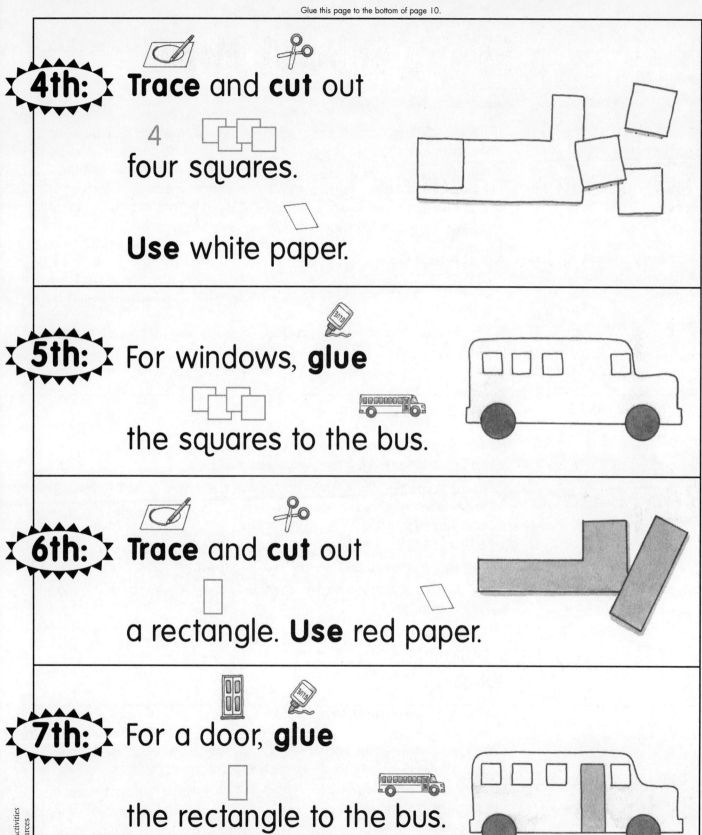

4th: **Trace** and **cut** out

4 four squares.

Use white paper.

5th: For windows, **glue**

the squares to the bus.

6th: **Trace** and **cut** out

a rectangle. **Use** red paper.

7th: For a door, **glue**

the rectangle to the bus.

Get on Board!

How to Make
an Apple Mobile

Getting Started

Invite children to share what they know about how and where apples grow. Then share a book about the growing cycle of an apple tree (see Literature Links, left). Discuss the changes an apple tree undergoes throughout the seasons, from blossoms in the spring to green leaves with small, green apples in the summer to big, ripe apples in the fall. Then tell students that they are each going to create a mobile to celebrate apples.

What You Need (for each child)

- Apple Mobile directions, pages 13–14
- apple patterns, page 25
- red construction paper, 8 by 9 inches
- yellow construction paper, 4 by 6 inches
- length of yarn, 18 inches
- glue
- green, light green, and brown construction paper scraps
- pencil
- scissors

Tips for Success

❋ Highlight the color words in the directions using markers in corresponding colors.

❋ In the third step, when students glue the apple parts onto the yarn, remind them to leave space between each part so that the parts will move freely.

❋ Instead of gluing the apple parts to the yarn, students can punch holes in each section and tie pieces of yarn between them.

❋ In the sixth step, students may need assistance tying a loop in the end of the yarn.

❋ Students can use brown or black crayons to add seeds to the cores of their apples, if they like.

Do More!

Taste, Compare, and Graph! (Math)

Ask students to bring in a variety of different types of apples. Red and Golden Delicious, Granny Smith, McIntosh, and Winesap are a few possibilities. (Go to **applesource.com** to see a listing of more than 100 varieties of apples! These are available for purchase during their growing season.)

Have a tasting party in which each child has an opportunity to taste all the different kinds. (Check for food allergies first.) Ask students to choose their favorites. Create a class graph with the results. Ask questions about the graph such as, "Which apple was the most popular? Least popular? Were any of the apples equally liked? Were there any that no one in the class chose as the favorite?" Discuss possible reasons why.

Literature Links

Apples by Gail Gibbons (Holiday House, 2000). This engaging nonfiction book includes historical facts about apples, and information about how apples grow, apple varieties, where apples are sold, and the many ways they are used.

Apple Picking Time by Michele Benoit Slawson (Dragonfly, 1998) At harvest time, Anna, her family, and the rest of her community work to help bring in the apple harvest. Young readers will identify with Anna's determination to fill a bin by herself.

The Apple Pie Tree by Zoe Hall (Blue Sky Press, 1996) Easy-to-read text paired with exuberant and colorful textured collages bring the growing cycle of an apple tree to life.

How to Make an Apple Mobile

1st:  **Trace** and **cut** out the top

and bottom of the apple.

Use red paper.

2nd: **Trace** and **cut** out

the center of the apple.

Use yellow paper.

3rd: **Glue** a piece of yarn

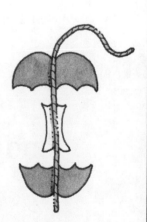

3

to the three parts.

Leave space between each part.

Cut off this bottom strip along the dotted line. Then glue this page to the top of page 14.

13

 4th: On scrap paper, **trace** and

cut out a stem, leaf, and worm.

Glue them to the apple.

Draw a face on the worm.

 5th: **Cut** off the extra yarn

from the bottom

of the apple.

 6th: **Tie** a loop at the top

end of the yarn.

Now hang your mobile!

14

Follow-the-Directions Art Activities Scholastic Teaching Resources

a Fire Safety Dog Puppet

Getting Started

Introduce a firefighter as a community worker. Talk about the special gear and equipment firefighters need to fight fires. Create riddle clues about specific pieces of equipment or things in a firehouse and see if students can guess what they are. Then lead into the art activity using the final riddle. (See examples, right.)

What You Need (for each child)

- Fire Safety Dog Puppet directions, pages 16–17
- fire hat patterns, page 26
- white construction paper, 5 by 5 inches
- red construction paper, 6 by 10 inches
- pencil
- scissors
- glue
- black marker
- wide craft stick

Tips for Success

❋ Use a red marker to highlight the word *red* in the third step.

❋ To build vocabulary, when students fold the square in half to make a triangle in the first step, you might tell them that another way to say this is, "Fold the square in half on the *diagonal*."

❋ Some students may need help with the fourth–sixth steps. (In the sixth step, direct students to glue the small hat pattern to the back of the larger one at the fold.) Create a sample for students to refer to as they make the hat, and then model each step for them.

Do More!

To observe National Fire Prevention Week in October, teach students about what to do in the event of a fire in their home. Include a discussion about calling 911 and these fire safety tips:

- In the event of a fire, don't hide. Leave the building.
- Get out of a smoke-filled room by crawling close to the floor, below the smoke.
- Touch doors to make sure they are not hot before opening them.
- Choose a safe family meeting place outside of the home.
- Check smoke alarms once a month.
- Practice Stop, Drop, and Roll—what to do if your clothes catch fire:
  Stop: Stop where you are. Don't run.
  Drop: Drop to the floor.
  Roll: Cover your face with your hands and roll over and over to put out the fire.
- Invite children to use their fire safety puppets in short plays that feature fire safety rules.

Firehouse Riddles

- It is hard.
  It might be red, black, or yellow.
  It is worn on a firefighter's head for protection.
  What is it?

  (Answer: helmet)

- They are rubber.
  A firefighter has two of these.
  They are worn on firefighters' feet to keep them safe and dry.
  What are they?

  (Answer: boots)

- You often see me at a firehouse.
  I am furry.
  I have spots.

  (Answer: A Dalmatian)

Literature Links

Firefighters A to Z by Chris Demarest (Margaret K. McElderry, 2000)
"A is for Alarm that rings loud and clear," is the first rhyming entry in this informative book about firefighters, the equipment they use, and the work that they do.

Fire! Fire! By Gail Gibbons (HarperTrophy, 1987)
A wonderful expository book about firefighters, fire trucks, and all the equipment necessary to fight fires.

How to Make
a Fire Safety Dog Puppet

1st: **Fold** the white square

$\frac{1}{2}$

in half, corner to corner,

to make a triangle.

This is your dog's head.

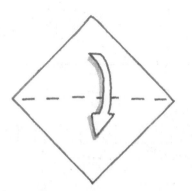

2nd: **Fold** down the top corners

to make ears.

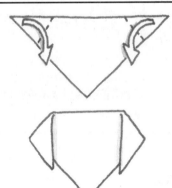

3rd: **Trace** and **cut** out

2

two fire hat patterns.

Use red paper.

Follow-the-Directions Art Activities   Scholastic Teaching Resources

 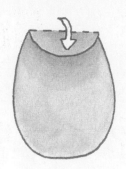

4th: **Fold** down the narrow end

of the LARGE hat pattern.

5th: **Glue** it to the back

of your dog's head.

 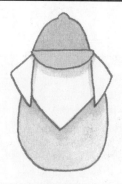

6th: **Glue** the small hat pattern

to the top of the large hat.

7th: **Draw** a face and spots.

8th: **Glue** the head

to a craft stick.

Arf! Arf! Where's the fire?

Follow-the-Directions Art Activities
Scholastic Teaching Resources

a Spider Headband

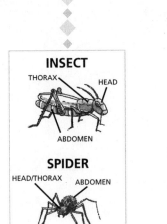

INSECT
THORAX
HEAD
ABDOMEN

SPIDER
HEAD/THORAX
ABDOMEN

Getting Started

What do students know about spiders? Have they ever seen one? Is a spider an insect? If possible, share books that have photographs of both spiders and insects. Then, on chart paper, draw simple diagrams of an insect and a spider (see left). Ask students to describe how the creatures are alike and different. For example, an insect has three distinct body parts: the *head*, *abdomen*, and *thorax*. A spider has only two parts: the head and thorax make up one part, and the abdomen the other. Also discuss the number of legs each has. (An insect has six legs while spiders have eight.) Then tell students that they are going to use what they learned about a spider's legs to make a wriggly spider they can wear.

What You Need (for each child)

- Spider Headband directions, pages 19–20
- spider body pattern, page 26
- gray construction paper, 6 by 6 inches
- pencil
- scissors

- black construction paper strip, 2¹/₂ by 24 inches
- glue
- black and red markers
- eight black construction paper strips, ³/₄ by 7 inches
- stapler

Tips for Success

❋ Highlight the color words in the directions using markers in corresponding colors.

❋ In the third step, when students draw a face on their spider, you might provide wiggle eyes for them to use instead.

❋ In the fifth step, students can make wide or narrow folds in the strips. Guide students to discover that the more narrow the folds, the springier their spider's legs will be.

❋ Assist students in fitting the headbands to their heads and stapling them closed.

Do More!

Read several nonfiction books about spiders to your class. Then encourage students to collect information and write facts about spiders. Culminate the learning by building your own class web. Sit with students in a circle. Hold a ball of yarn in one hand and the end of the yarn in the other. Throw the ball to a child while holding onto the end. Before throwing the ball to another child, the student must state one fact he or she has learned about spiders. When the ball is passed to other students, children should continue to hold on to their section of yarn with one hand. Continue passing the yarn and sharing spider facts until you and your students have created an intricate yarn web.

a Spider Headband

   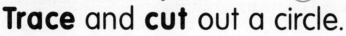 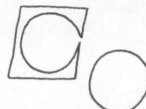

1st:  **Trace** and **cut** out a circle.

Use gray paper.

 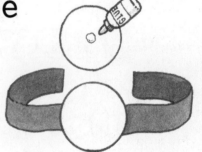

2nd: **Glue** the middle of the circle

to the middle

of the LARGE black strip.

3rd: **Draw** a face on the circle.

 8

4th:  **Count** eight small black strips.

Cut off this bottom strip along the dotted line. Then glue this page to the top of page 20.

19

Follow-the-Directions Art Activities   Scholastic Teaching Resources

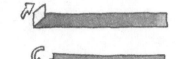

5th:  **Fold** the strips

back and forth like a fan.

6th: **Glue** four strips 4

under each side

of the spider's face.

These are its legs.

7th: **Fit** the headband

to your head.

Staple it closed.

Now wear your wiggly spider!

Follow-the-Directions Art Activities Scholastic Teaching Resources

How to Make
a Fold-Up Turkey

Getting Started

Discuss the Thanksgiving traditions your students celebrate. Ask questions such as, "Does your family celebrate Thanksgiving? If so, where will you celebrate Thanksgiving this year? With whom do you celebrate?" Share with them your family's traditions, too. Also encourage students to describe the kinds of foods their families traditionally eat for Thanksgiving dinner. On chart paper, list children's responses. Challenge students to sort these foods into the food groups on the Food Pyramid. (For a full-color poster of the Pyramid that you can print out, go to: **www.nal.usda.gov/fnic/Fpyr/pyramid.html**.) Then tell students that they are each going to make a Thanksgiving turkey to help celebrate this national holiday.

What You Need (for each child)

- Fold-Up Turkey directions, pages 22–23
- brown construction paper square, 8 by 8 inches
- crayons
- scrap paper
- glue
- decorating materials (craft feathers, yarn, wiggle eyes, colored paper scraps, and so on)

Tips for Success

✽ In the first step, highlight the word *brown* using a brown marker.

✽ Children might like to add details to their turkey, such as a construction paper wattle or feathers for the tail. Provide craft materials for them to use.

✽ Invite children to make additional fold-up turkeys to use as place cards on their family's Thanksgiving table. Have them write the name of each family member on a slip of paper, tape it under the turkey's beak or on its tail, and then put a turkey at each place setting.

Do More!

Share some stories about turkeys that are spared and invited to Thanksgiving dinner as guests (see Literature Links, right). Tell children to pretend they are turkeys. Have them each write a letter to a cook, asking not to be eaten, giving reasons why they should be spared. Encourage students to be funny and zany!

Literature Links

Gracias, the Thanksgiving Turkey by Joy Cowley (Scholastic, 1996) Spanish text mingles with English in this story of Miguel, who befriends the turkey his father bought for Thanksgiving dinner.

Sometimes It's Turkey, Sometimes It's Feathers by Lorna Balian and Lecia Balian (Star Bright Books, 2003; revised) A delightful story about a turkey that escapes the ax and becomes a guest at Thanksgiving dinner.

'Twas the Night Before Thanksgiving by Dav Pilkey (Orchard Books, 1990) A group of school children devise a plan to save the turkeys on Farmer Mack Nugget's turkey farm from their Thanksgiving fate.

How to Make
a Fold-Up Turkey

 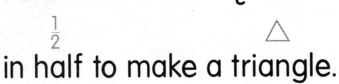 

1st: **Fold** the brown square

$\frac{1}{2}$ △

in half to make a triangle.

 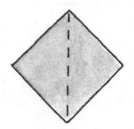

Then **unfold** it.

2nd: **Fold** in the two corners

2

on each side so they

meet in the middle.

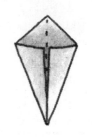

3rd: Now **fold** in

2

the two new corners

to the middle, too.

Cut off this bottom strip along the dotted line. Then glue this page to the top of page 23.

Follow-the-Directions Art Activities   Scholastic Teaching Resources

 **Fold** the thin, bottom point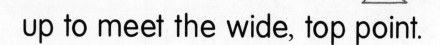

up to meet the wide, top point.

 **Fold** the thin point down.

This is your turkey's head.

 **Fold** the wide point up.

This is your turkey's tail.

 **Decorate** your turkey using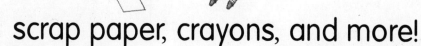

scrap paper, crayons, and more!

Gobble! Gobble!

Follow-the-Directions Art Activities
Scholastic Teaching Resources

door

bus

window

wheel

apple top

apple bottom

leaf

apple middle

stem

worm

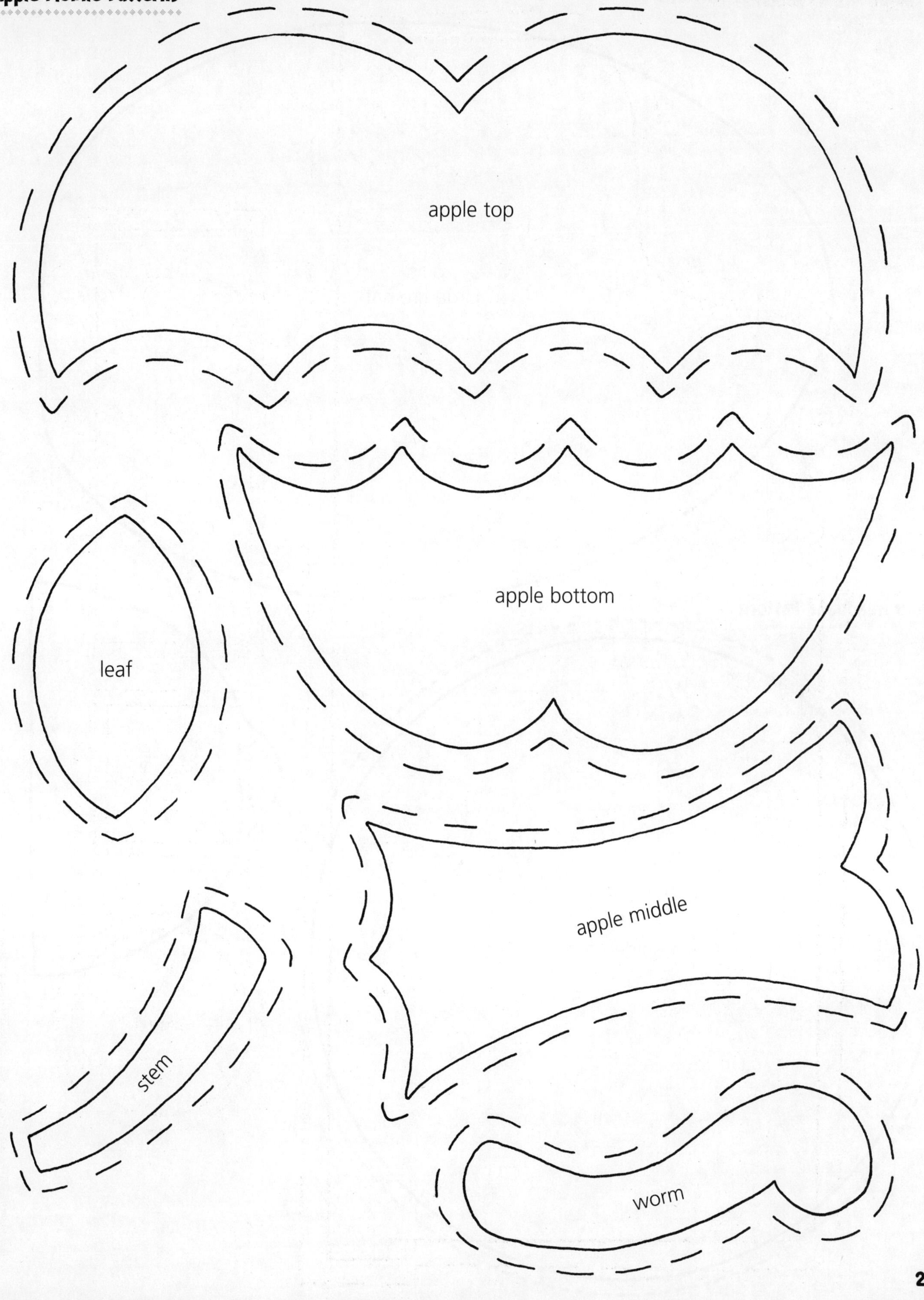

large fire hat

Spider Headband Pattern

spider face

small
fire hat

 **How to Make**

a Snowman Ornament

Getting Started

What kinds of activities do students enjoy during the winter months? Having a snowball fight? Ice skating? Sledding? Building a snow fort or a snowman? Take a survey of the class to find out which winter activity is the most popular. If it does not snow where you live, invite children to name the winter activity they would most *like* to do and explain why. To build background knowledge, share books that describe and show what snowy winters are like. Then tell children they are going to make a snowman that won't melt—ever!

What You Need (for each child)

- Snowman Ornament directions, pages 28–29
- snowman hat pattern, page 42
- black construction paper, 3 by 4 inches
- pencil
- scissors

- wide craft stick, painted white
- glue
- orange construction paper, 1 by 1 inch
- black marker
- assorted small buttons
- length of red or green ribbon, 5 inches

Tips for Success

✢ Ahead of time, paint the craft sticks white or have students do this as part of the activity. Use the pictures and labels on page 81, to add these directions.

✢ Highlight the color words in the directions using markers in corresponding colors.

✢ You may want to precut the paper hats and noses ahead of time. Substitute craft foam for the construction paper, if desired.

✢ Wire or twisted ribbon (available at craft stores) work well for the scarf because the materials they are made of are somewhat stiff; the scarf will look like it's blowing in the wind!

✢ After students have completed their snowman, punch a small hole in the snowman's hat and add a loop of thin ribbon so that students may hang it on their Christmas tree. If students do not celebrate Christmas, attach a strip of magnetic tape to the back so it can become a refrigerator magnet.

Do More!

Have your students think about a time when they built a snowman (or what it would be like to build one.) Talk about the materials and steps needed to create a snowman. Then give students practice in procedural writing by asking them to describe, step by step, how to build a snowman. Encourage them to include illustrations with their directions.

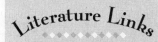 *Literature Links*

The Biggest, Best Snowman by Margery Cuyler (Scholastic, 1998) Nell tries to help with the planning of a party but is told that she's too small. She then heads to the woods and, with the help of her woodland friends, builds a great big snowman to prove she is not too small at all!

The Snowman by Raymond Briggs (Random House, 1978) This wordless book tells the story of what happens when a snowman comes alive one night. The snowman learns about life indoors when he visits the boy who made him earlier that day.

a Snowman Ornament

1st: **Trace** and **cut** out a hat.

Use black paper.

2nd: **Glue** the hat

to the craft stick.

3rd: For a nose, **cut** out

a small **triangle**.

Use orange paper.

4th:  **Glue** the nose

to the craft stick.

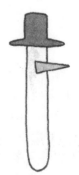

Follow-the-Directions Art Activities Scholastic Teaching Resources

Cut off this bottom strip along the dotted line. Then glue this page to the top of page 29.

5th:  **Draw** two eyes

and a mouth.

6th:  **Glue** three buttons

to the craft stick.

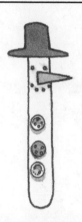

7th: For a scarf, **choose**

red or green ribbon.

Tie the ribbon

on your snowman.

Hello, snowman!

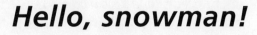

29

a Peace Dove

Getting Started

Share with students books about the life of Dr. Martin Luther King, Jr. (see Literature Links, left). Then discuss situations that Martin Luther King, Jr., and other African Americans encountered in the past, such as not being allowed to attend school with white children, or not being permitted to use certain restrooms or restaurants or sit in certain seats on the bus. Discuss how Martin Luther King, Jr., fought peacefully to do away with these forms of discrimination and to create new laws under which all people were treated fairly. Compare what it was like to live during the time of Dr. King to what it's like today. Then tell students that to commemorate the life and work of Dr. King, they are going to make a white dove, a symbol of peace and cooperation.

What You Need (for each child)

- Peace Dove directions, pages 31–32
- large white paper plate
- scissors
- glue
- decorating materials (colored paper scraps, wiggle eyes, crayons, craft feathers, glitter glue, and so on)

Tips for Success

❋ In the first through third steps, check that students cut the pieces in half, along the fold.

❋ To build math vocabulary, introduce the term *one-fourth* when students complete the third step.

❋ After students glue the tail, head, and wing to the bird's body in the fourth, fifth, and sixth steps, make sure they let the glue dry completely before decorating their bird.

Do More!

Talk with students about hypothetical situations and ask them to decide if people were or were not treated fairly. Begin with generic situations that children are familiar with, such as being excluded from a game that other students are playing, or being mistakenly blamed for cheating. To allow students to indicate their responses nonverbally, give each of them a card with a simple happy face on one side and a sad face on the other (or have children show their opinion with a "thumbs up" or "thumbs down"). Then pose other situations for students to consider, such as those from current events, and let children indicate their opinion. Afterward, encourage children to explain the reasoning for their opinions and to share why they feel this way.

How to Make
a Peace Dove

 **1st:** **Fold** a paper plate in half.

Cut the plate in half.

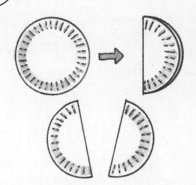

 **2nd:** **Fold** one piece in half.

Cut this piece in half.

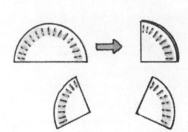

 **3rd:** **Fold** one small piece in half.

Then **cut** it in half.

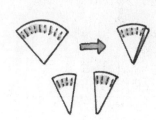

 **4th:** For a tail, **glue** one

of the very small pieces

to one side of the half plate.

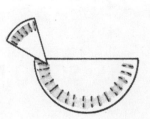

Cut off this bottom strip along the dotted line. Then glue this page to the top of page 32.

31

5th:  For a head, **glue**

the other very small **piece**

to the opposite side.

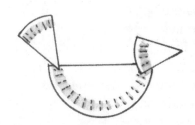

6th: For a wing, **glue**

the last piece on top.

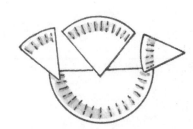

7th: **Decorate** your bird using

 scrap paper, crayons, and more!

Tweet! Tweet!

32

Follow-the-Directions Art Activities Scholastic Teaching Resources

 How to Make

a Cotton Swab Snowflake

Getting Started

Before beginning this activity, ask students, "Did you know that no two snowflakes are alike?" Because of the way a snowflake, or snow crystal, is formed, it is highly unlikely that there are two that are exactly the same. This is also true of other things in the world. Challenge children to think of other examples. Examples might include people, trees, clouds, and rocks. Begin a list of the items your class generated and keep it posted in your room. As your students think of other examples, add them to your list. You will be surprised at what they think of!

What You Need (for each child)

• Cotton Swab Snowflake directions, pages 34–35
• cotton swabs
• scissors
• wax paper, 6 by 6 inches
• glue
• permanent marker
• glitter (optional)

Tips for Success

❋ Before beginning this project, review with students the concept of repeating patterns, and provide a few examples.

❋ In the third step, have students make a pool of glue about the size of a quarter on the waxed paper. The pool needs to be just big enough so that all of the ends of the cotton swabs touch the glue. This will make sure that all of the swabs are anchored when the glue dries.

❋ Have students use a permanent marker to write their names on the wax paper squares.

❋ To make their snowflakes sparkle, students can dab glue on different parts of the swabs and then sprinkle them with glitter.

❋ Even if it doesn't snow where you live, make it snow in your classroom! Hang the snowflakes from the ceiling using fishing line, hung at various lengths.

Do More!

Continue to explore repeating patterns with your students. Ask them to look at the cotton swab snowflakes they made. Help them identify the types of patterns they created (AB, AAB, ABB, and so on), and then come up with patterns that are not represented. Afterward, invite children to make additional cotton swab snowflakes using these new patterns.

How to Make
a Cotton Swab Snowflake

 **Choose** some cotton swabs.

 $\frac{1}{2}$

Cut some of them in half.

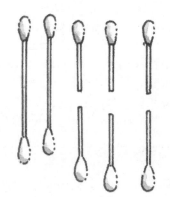

 **Think** about how

 snowflakes look.

Practice making

a snowflake pattern

using the cotton swabs.

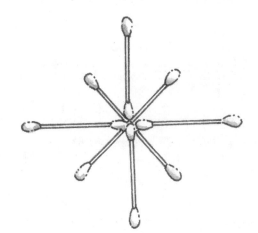

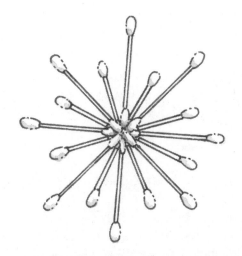

Follow-the-Directions Art Activities   Scholastic Teaching Resources

3rd: **Squeeze** a pool of glue

in the middle

of the waxed paper.

4th: **Make** your snowflake pattern.

Place each cotton swab

on the waxed paper

with one end in the glue.

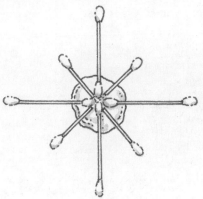

5th: Let the glue dry.

Peel off the waxed paper.

Let it snow!

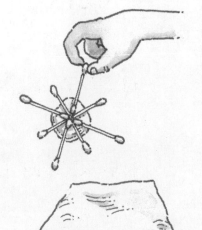

Follow-the-Directions Art Activities
Scholastic Teaching Resources

How to Make a Valentine Mouse

The Best Valentine in the World
by Marjorie Weinman Sharmat
(Holiday House, 1982)
Children will get in the mood
to create their own valentines
as they read about Ferdinand
Fox's determination to make a
valentine for his sweetheart,
Florette.

Frederick by Leo Lionni
(Pantheon, 1967)
Frederick, a field mouse,
shares dreams and memories
to cheer his friends during
the long winter. Other classic
books about mice by Leo
Lionni include *Nicolas,
Where Have You Been?,
Alexander and the Wind-Up
Mouse,* and *A Busy Year.*

*If You Give a Mouse a
Cookie* by Laura Joffe Numeroff
(HarperCollins, 1985)
Children will love this funny
circle story about a mouse
who continues to want more:
He wants scissors to trim his
hair, a straw to drink his
milk, a magnet to hang his
picture on the refrigerator,
and more!

Literature Links

Getting Started

Use this adorable mouse to welcome Valentine's Day and teach a lesson on symmetry. Introduce the topic by showing children pictures of symmetrical objects, such as feathers, leaves, and butterflies. Ask students what they notice about each of these items (*each side looks just like the other*). Then provide students with simple shapes cut from paper (a triangle, a leaf, a shell, a mitten, an irregular blob, a shoe). Explain that if they fold a shape that is symmetrical along its line of symmetry, its two sides will match up exactly. Model how to fold one of the shapes to see whether or not it is symmetrical. Then have students practice folding the shapes and sorting them into two groups, "symmetrical" and "not symmetrical."

What You Need (for each child)

- Valentine Mouse directions, pages 37–38
- mouse patterns, page 42
- pencil
- scissors
- pink construction paper, 9 by 9 inches
- red construction paper, 3 by 3 inches
- glue
- black and pink or red markers
- length of red curling ribbon, 6 to 8 inches

Tips for Success

❋ Highlight the color words in the directions using markers in corresponding colors.

❋ For the second step, model how to fold the heart in half on the line of symmetry (vertically). Some children may need assistance.

❋ Students can glue wiggle eyes to their mouse instead of drawing eyes, and use yarn instead of ribbon for the tail.

❋ Children will discover a surprise when they complete this project— their mouse can rock back and forth!

❋ Invite students to write a valentine message inside their mouse and give it to a family member or special friend.

❋ For another activity that involves symmetry, see How to Make a Beautiful Butterfly, page 66.

Do More!

Measure Mouse Tails! (Math)
Have a variety of lengths of ribbon or yarn available for the tails. Invite children to measure the mouse tails using nonstandard units such as paper clips or rubber bands or standard units such as inches or centimeters. Discuss why the results differ depending on the size of the unit used to measure.

How to Make
a Valentine Mouse

1st:

Trace and **cut** out

one LARGE heart.

Use pink paper.

2nd:

Fold the heart in half.

This is your mouse.

3rd:

Trace and **cut** out

two small hearts.

Use red paper.

 **4th:**  **Glue** the red hearts to

 each side of your mouse

to make ears.

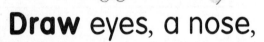 **Draw** eyes, a nose,

 **5th:**

 a mouth, and whiskers.

Glue a ribbon

 **6th:** to your mouse.

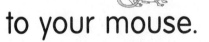

Now it has a tail.

Happy Valentine's Day!

How to Make
a Pair of Mittens

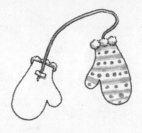

Getting Started

Brrr! Winter brings cold weather. Ask students to name types of clothing that are appropriate for cold weather. (*hats, scarves, heavy coats, and mittens!*) What's special about mittens? They come in pairs. Continue the discussion by talking about other items of clothing that come in pairs. Ask students to think of items that fall into this category. (*for example, socks, shoes, gloves, boots, and skates*) What sometimes happens to clothing that comes in pairs? One item in the pair can get lost! Tell students that they are going to make a pair of mittens in such a way that neither one can get lost.

What You Need (for each child)

- Pair of Mittens directions, pages 40–41
- construction paper, assorted colors, 9 by 12 inches
- pencil
- scissors
- crayons
- six cotton balls
- glue
- length of yarn, about 20 inches

Tips for Success

✳ Model the first through fourth steps for students. Show them that when you fold a sheet of paper in half and then cut out a shape, you will then have two shapes.

✳ In the fifth step, before students decorate their mittens, point out to them that they need to position the mittens so that the thumbs on each point inward.

✳ In the sixth step, when students glue the cotton balls to their mittens, you might want to introduce the word *cuff*.

Do More!

Here are some fun, learning-rich ideas for using the classic tale *The Mitten*:

- Share with students two versions of the story (see Literature Links, right). Then help them compare the two versions using a Venn diagram. You may choose to focus on the characters, setting, or problem and solution in each story.

- Have students sequence the characters on a sequence chain. To do this, have them work with a partner. One child sequences the first version's characters in the order in which they appear, while the other child sequences the characters in the second version.

- This is a favorite story for children to dramatize. Invite students to retell the story by acting it out.

Literature Links

Share these retellings of an old Ukrainian folktale in which a boy loses his mitten while out in the snow and several animals crawl inside it to keep warm in the cold.

The Mitten retold by Alvin Tresselt (Mulberry Books, 1989)

The Mitten retold by Jan Brett (Scholastic Books, 1990)

The Woodcutter's Mitten retold by Loek Koopmans (Crocodile Books, 1995) Check your library or online sources for this version.

How to Make
a Pair of Mittens

1st: **Fold** a piece of paper

$\frac{1}{2}$ in half the short way.

You **choose** the color.

2nd: **Lay** your hand on the paper.

Keep your fingers together

and your thumb apart.

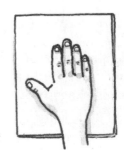

3rd: **Trace** around your hand.

4th: **Cut** out the two 2

mitten shapes.

Cut off this bottom strip along the dotted line. Then glue this page to the top of page 41.

Follow-the-Directions Art Activities   Scholastic Teaching Resources

 **Think** of a pattern

to put on your mittens.

Draw the pattern

on your mittens.

 **Glue** three cotton balls

to the bottom of each mitten.

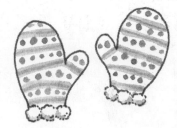

 **Tape** the end

of a piece of yarn

to the back of each mitten.

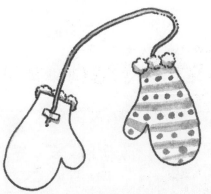

Bundle up!

Valentine Mouse Patterns

Snowman Ornament Pattern

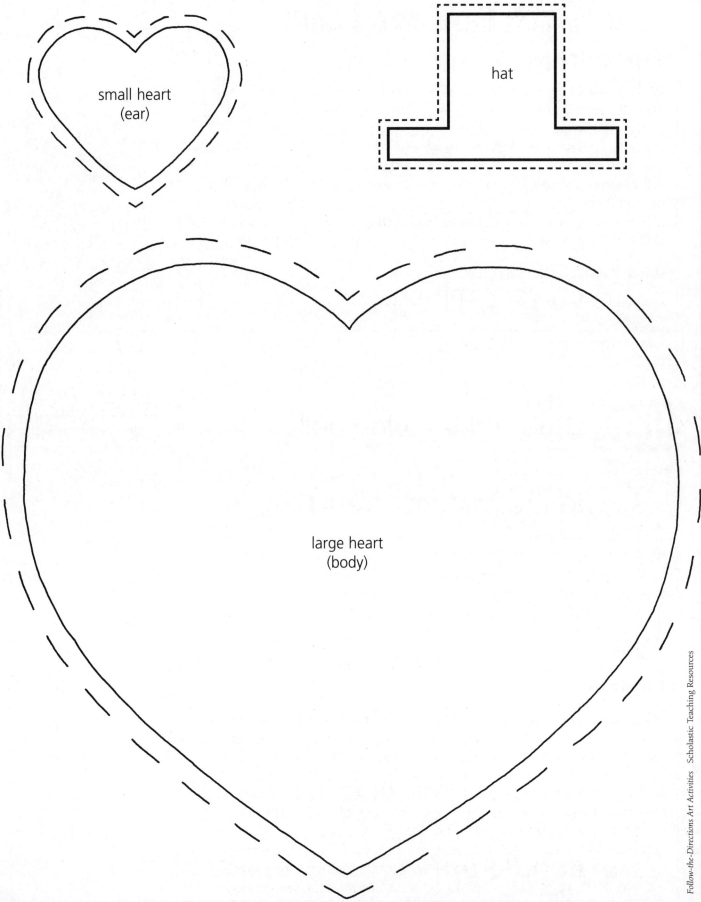

small heart
(ear)

hat

large heart
(body)

Follow-the-Directions Art Activities Scholastic Teaching Resources

How to Make
a March Lion and Lamb

Getting Started

At the beginning of the month of March, write the saying
"March comes in like a lion and goes out like a lamb"
on the chalkboard. Read aloud the sentence and then ask
if anyone knows what it means. Explain that March is
the time when the seasons change from winter to spring.
People long ago compared the blustery, cold weather in early March to that
of a lion's roar. They thought of the calmer, milder weather typical of late
March as being like a lamb. Tell children that they are going to make a March
Lion and Lamb puppet that they can use to monitor the month's weather.

What You Need (for each child)

- March Lion and Lamb directions, pages 44–45
- large white paper plate
- black marker
- yellow construction paper strips, 1 by 6 inches
- orange construction paper strips, 1 by 6 inches
- pencil
- glue
- cotton balls

Tips for Success

❋ Highlight the color words in the directions using markers in corresponding colors.

❋ In the second step, check that students draw the lamb's face so it is right side up behind the lion's.

❋ Some children may need assistance rolling the strips around a pencil to make the curly strips.

❋ Punch a hole through the top of children's plates and hang with a piece of yarn so that both faces can be displayed.

❋ Make an extra project to display on a bulletin board. Each day, let children take turns choosing the face that best reflects the weather.

Do More!

Ask children to predict how many "lion" and "lamb" days there will be
in March. Make a chart that shows each child's predictions. Each day of
the month, ask children to hold up their puppet so that either the lion or the
lamb faces out, depending on the weather. Have children take turns
drawing either a lion or a lamb on the calendar. (You might also have each
child keep a weather journal by giving each a copy of a blank calendar to
complete. Have students fill in the dates on their calendars first.) At the end
of the month, tally or graph the results from the calendar, recording the
number each of lion and lamb days. Have students compare their predictions
with the actual data. How would students comment on the saying now?

Literature Links

On the Same Day in March: A Tour of the World's Weather by Marilyn Singer (HarperTrophy, 2001). From Paris to Patagonia, this engaging book takes readers on a tour around the planet to discover what the weather is like in 17 different places "on the same day in March."

Weather Forecasting by Gail Gibbons (Atheneum, 1987) How do weather forecasters predict the weather? Young readers get an inside look at the workings of a weather station.

How to Make
a March Lion and Lamb

1st:  **Draw** a lion's face

on the paper plate.

2nd:  **Draw** a lamb's face

on the back of the plate.

3rd:  **Make** curly strips.

Roll yellow and orange strips

around a pencil.

(Cut off this bottom strip along the dotted line. Then glue this page to the top of page 45.)

Follow-the-Directions Art Activities   Scholastic Teaching Resources

 **4th:** **Make** your lion's mane.

Glue the curly strips

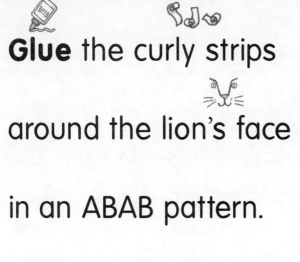

around the lion's face

in an ABAB pattern.

Let the glue dry.

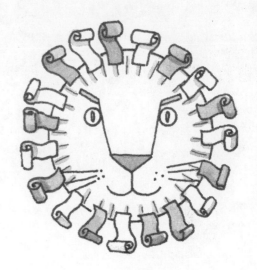

 **5th:** **Make** your lamb's wool.

Glue cotton balls

around the lamb's face.

What's the weather like today?

A lion or a lamb?

45

How to Make a Wind Sock

Literature Links

Feel the Wind by Arthur Dorros (Crowell, 1989) Through easy-to-read text, readers learn the causes of wind, its effects, and how people use it.

Jack and the Whoopee Wind by Mary Calhoun (HarperCollins, 1987) Check your library or online book sources for this rollicking tall tale about Jack's efforts to tame the wild Whoopee Wind that is raising havoc on his farm.

The Wind Blew by Pat Hutchins (Aladdin, 1993) In this humorous rhyming story, the wind is making mischief, making off with hats, umbrellas, letters, and even a wig!

Getting Started

Begin by asking students, "What is wind?" or "What does wind look like?" Explain that wind is moving air. Discuss the fact that although we cannot actually see the wind, we are able to see its effects in the form of leaves blowing or a kite flying. Ask students to name other examples that indicate the wind is blowing. Then tell them that they are going to make a device called a wind sock that they can use to see from which direction and how hard the wind is blowing.

What You Need (for each child)

- Wind Sock directions, pages 47–48
- tagboard, 6 by 18 inches
- construction paper strips, assorted colors, 1 by 18 inches
- glue
- stapler
- tissue paper strips, assorted colors and lengths, about 1 inch wide
- hole punch
- length of yarn, about 12 inches

Tips for Success

❋ In the second step, students should line up the strips close together on the tagboard before they apply glue.

❋ In the third step, check that students roll the tagboard into a cylinder, striped side facing out.

❋ In the sixth step, students may need assistance tying the ends of the yarn through the holes in their wind sock.

Do More!

Introduce students to the Beaufort Scale, a measure meteorologists use to find out how hard the wind is blowing. Simplify the scale to meet your students' abilities. For example, 0 might represent no wind, 1 a slight breeze, 2 some wind, and 3 a strong wind. Take students outdoors with their wind socks to observe and measure the wind's force. By observing the movement of the streamers on the wind socks, students can determine how hard or softly the wind is blowing. Set up a "wind calendar" on which your class can record their findings daily for one to two weeks. At the end of this time, talk with students about the wind patterns that they noticed.

How to Make a Wind Sock

1st:  **Count** six strips of paper.

Choose different colors.

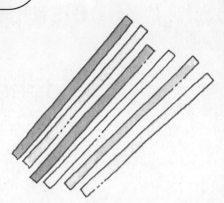

2nd:  **Glue** the strips

side by side

to the tagboard.

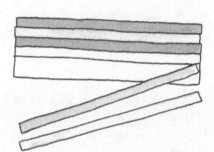

3rd: **Roll** the tagboard

into a cylinder.

 Staple it closed at the top,

the bottom, and the middle.

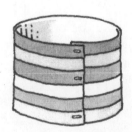

4th: **Glue** strips of tissue paper

around the bottom

of the cylinder, on the inside.

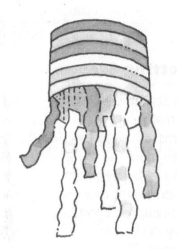

5th: **Punch** two holes

on opposite sides

of the cylinder, near the top.

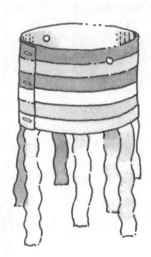

6th: **Poke** the ends of the yarn

through each hole.

Make two knots.

Blow, wind, blow!

48

Follow-the-Directions Art Activities Scholastic Teaching Resources

a Lucky Leprechaun

Getting Started

On St. Patrick's Day, before students arrive, use washable paint to make little green footprints around your classroom. Knock over a few items and leave a letter for your class from "Lucky the Leprechaun." For even more fun, put out green juice (add a few drops of blue and yellow food coloring); green munchies, such as celery sticks, green pepper rings, and green beans; or sweet treats in the form of green jelly beans and gold, foil-wrapped chocolate coins, from Lucky's pot of gold! Tell students that a very clever little leprechaun visited their classroom and that they are going to make their very own today.

What You Need (for each child)

- Lucky Leprechaun directions, pages 50–52
- leprechaun patterns, pages 60–61
- pencil
- scissors
- green construction paper, 9 by 12 inches
- two yellow and two orange construction paper strips, 1 by 12 inches
- two yellow and two orange construction paper strips, 1 by 6 inches
- black construction paper, 5 by 7 inches
- glue
- crayons

Tips for Success

❈ Highlight the color words in the directions using markers in corresponding colors.

❈ In the second step, provide two colors of long and short strips to give students a choice.

❈ In the third step, students can make wide or narrow folds in the strips. Guide them to discover that the more narrow the folds, the springier their leprechaun's arms and legs will be.

❈ In the fourth and fifth steps, when students add the arms and legs, direct them to glue them to the back of the shamrock, for a cleaner look.

❈ In the last step, when students draw Lucky's face, you might provide wiggle eyes and other decorating materials for them to use, if desired.

Do More!

After reading books about leprechauns to your class (see Literature Links, right), students will be excited to search for and catch their very own leprechaun! Remind them that, according to legend, once you catch a leprechaun, it is very difficult to trick him into telling you where he has hidden his gold. Have students write letters to a leprechaun persuading him to tell them where his gold is hidden. If students are unfamiliar with letter writing, take some time to teach them about the parts of a friendly letter.

Literature Links

Clever Tom and the Leprechaun by Linda Shute (Lothrop, Lee & Shepard, 1988) Tom finds a leprechaun and thinks he has found a way to get his gold, but the little leprechaun proves to be a bit trickier.

Fluffy's Lucky Day by Kate McMullan (Cartwheel Books, 2003) In his dream, Fluffy meets a leprechaun who tries to trick him. But when he wakes up, Fluffy finds something even more exciting waiting for him, and St. Patrick's Day turns out lucky for Fluffy after all.

St. Patrick's Day in the Morning by Eve Bunting (Houghton Mifflin, 1980) Jamie's family is going to be in the St. Patrick's Day parade, but not Jamie—he's too small. So what does Jamie do? He takes part in a parade of his own.

How to Make a Lucky Leprechaun

1st:  **Trace** and **cut** out

1 one LARGE shamrock.

 **Use** green paper.

2nd: **Count** two L O N G

2

and two short paper strips.

Choose yellow or orange.

3rd: **Fold** each strip

 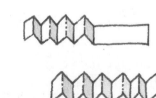

back and forth like a fan.

Cut off this bottom strip along the dotted line. Then glue this page to the top of page 51.

Follow-the-Directions Art Activities Scholastic Teaching Resources

4th: For arms, **glue**

2 two short strips

to the shamrock.

 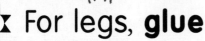

5th: For legs, **glue**

2 two L O N G strips

to the shamrock.

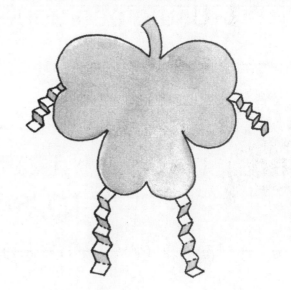

6th: **Trace** and **cut** out

4 four small **shamrocks**.

Use green paper.

Follow-the-Directions Art Activities
Scholastic Teaching Resources

Cut off this bottom strip along the dotted line. Then glue this page to the top of page 52.

51

**7th:** For hands and feet,

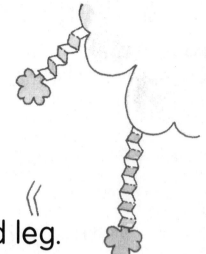

glue one small **shamrock**

to the end of each arm and leg.

**8th:** **Trace** and **cut** out a hat.

Use black paper.

**9th:** **Glue** the hat on top.

Draw a face.

Happy St. Patrick's Day!

Follow-the-Directions Art Activities   Scholastic Teaching Resources

a Bunny Bag Puppet

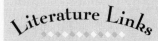

Getting Started

Before students make these projects, help them complete a Knowledge Chart about rabbits. On a large sheet of chart paper, prepare a T-chart. On one side, write "Old Knowledge" and on the other, write "New Knowledge." First ask children to share what they already know about rabbits and bunnies. Write students' responses on the "Old Knowledge" side. Then read a few informational books about rabbits to your class (see Literature Links, right). Afterward, ask them to complete the "New Knowledge" side. Revisit the first column and ask students whether they would like to change anything written there based on new information that they learned about rabbits. Then tell them to get ready to make their own hip-hoppity bunny!

What You Need (for each child)

- Bunny Bag Puppet directions, pages 54–56
- bunny patterns, page 61
- pencil
- scissors
- white construction paper, 9 by 9 inches
- pink construction paper, 4 by 4 inches
- glue
- white paper lunch bag
- black marker
- cotton ball

Tips for Success

❊ Highlight the color words in the directions using markers in corresponding colors.

❊ In the fourth step, students should glue the ears to the back of the flap on the bag.

❊ After students complete their puppets, encourage them to work together in groups to make up a skit about rabbits. Have them use their puppets to perform it for the class.

Do More!

Invite students to practice "hopping" like a bunny and help them build their measuring skills at the same time. Tell students to try to hop as far as they can. Record the distance for each child using a piece of masking tape. Then have students measure how far they jumped using nonstandard units such as blocks, pencils, feet, or hands. They may also work with standard measurements. Choose one type of unit and create a class graph displaying the results. Encourage children to analyze the results by asking questions such as, "Who hopped the longest distance? Who hopped the shortest distance?" and "Did any students hop equal distances? How do you know this?" Extend their thinking by exploring the differences in results for the different units used to measure.

Literature Links

Use the following books to help students learn about the life cycle, habits, and physical characteristics of rabbits, and what kinds make good pets.

The *Life Cycle of a Rabbit* by Lisa Trumbauer (Pebble Books, 2003)

Rabbits (First Step Nonfiction series) by Melanie S. Mitchell (Lerner, 2003)

Rabbit (Watch Me Grow series) by Lisa Magloff (Dorling Kindersley, 2004)

Rabbits by Fiona Patchett (Usborne, 1999)

How to Make
a Bunny Bag Puppet

1st: **Trace** and **cut** out

2

two LARGE ears.

Use white paper.

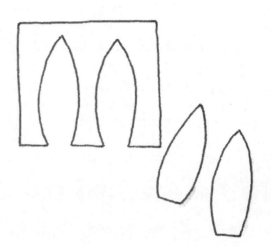

2nd: **Trace** and **cut** out

2

two small ears.

Use pink paper.

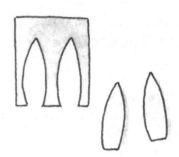

3rd: **Glue** the pink ears

to the white ears.

54   Cut off this bottom strip along the dotted line. Then glue this page to the top of page 55.

Follow-the-Directions Art Activities Scholastic Teaching Resources

4th: **Glue** the ears

to the back of the bag.

5th: **Trace** and **cut** out

two arms and two feet.

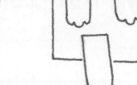

Use white paper.

6th: **Glue** the arms

to the front of the bag.

Glue the feet

to the bottom of the bag,

on the inside.

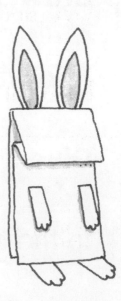

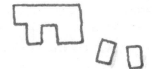

7th: **Trace** and **cut** out

2 two teeth.

Use white paper.

8th: **Glue** the teeth

under the flap on the bag.

9th: **Draw** a face.

Add whiskers.

Glue a cotton ball tail

to the back of your bunny!

Hippity-hop!

Follow-the-Directions Art Activities Scholastic Teaching Resources

How to Make
an Umbrella Flower

Getting Started

As spring arrives, we often hear people say, "April showers bring May Flowers." Write this saying on the chalkboard. Read it aloud and then ask if anyone knows what it means. Explain that the month of April is often rainy—but that this helps flowers to grow in May. Then tell children that they will celebrate this saying by making a flower that's also an umbrella!

What You Need (for each child)

- Umbrella Flower directions, pages 58–59
- flower patterns, page 62
- pencil
- scissors
- green construction paper, 4 by 8 inches
- brown construction paper, 5 by 5 inches
- blue construction paper, 12 by 12 inches
- construction paper, assorted colors, 6 by 9 inches
- glue

Tips for Success

❋ Highlight the color words in the directions using markers in corresponding colors.

❋ In the sixth step, remind students that they should glue only the flap, and not the entire umbrella to the stem.

❋ On the outside of the umbrella, invite students to write "April showers bring . . ."and then lift the flap to write "May flowers!"

❋ Students may enjoy making additional umbrella flowers to use as greeting cards for friends or relatives and writing personal messages under the flaps.

Do More!

Bring spring into your classroom! Buy some narcissus or paperwhite bulbs to grow with your students. Have children make predictions about how long it will take until they bloom (about one month), what color they will be, and how tall they will grow. Periodically, have students measure and record their growth on a chart. Have them use a variety of standard units (inches or centimeters) and nonstandard units (links or paper clips) to measure the flowers' heights. Compare how the results differ when using different units of measurements.

Literature Links

Grandma Fina and Her Wonderful Umbrellas/La Abuelita Fina y sus sombrillas maravillosas by Benjamin Alire Saenz (Cinco Puntos Press, 2001) Check your library or online book sources for this sweet story in English, with Spanish phrases sprinkled throughout. Grandma Fina loves her old yellow umbrella and enjoys walking with it. Readers will enjoy predicting what will happen when each of her neighbors thinks that she needs a new one.

Rain Talk by Mary Serfozo (Simon & Schuster, 1990) Over the course of a rainy day, a young girl experiences the many sounds that rain makes.

The Umbrella Party by Janet Lunn (Groundwood Books, 1998) A little girl's beautiful collection of umbrellas helps her celebrate her rainy birthday.

How to Make
an Umbrella Flower

1st: **Trace** and **cut** out

1   2   one stem and two leaves.

Use green paper.

2nd:  **Trace** and **cut** out

1   J   one handle.

Use brown paper.

3rd:  **Glue** the handle and stem

to blue paper. **Glue** the leaves

near the top of the stem.

Follow-the-Directions Art Activities Scholastic Teaching Resources

4th: **Trace** and **cut** out

 one paper umbrella.

You **choose** the color.

5th: **Fold** down the flap

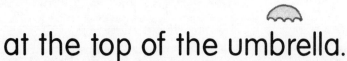 at the top of the umbrella.

6th: **Glue** the umbrella's flap

to the top of the stem.

Now you have a flower!

Fold down the umbrella.

You're ready for the rain!

small shamrock
(hands and feet)

large shamrock
(body)

Lucky Leprechaun Patterns

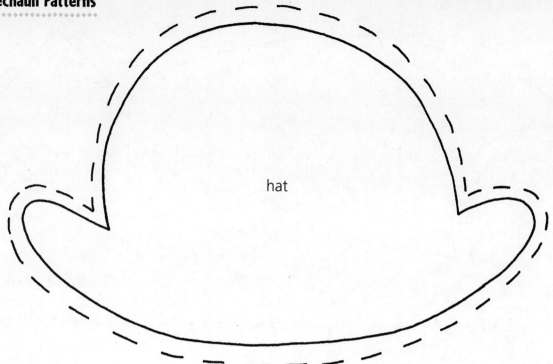

hat

Bunny Bag Puppet Patterns

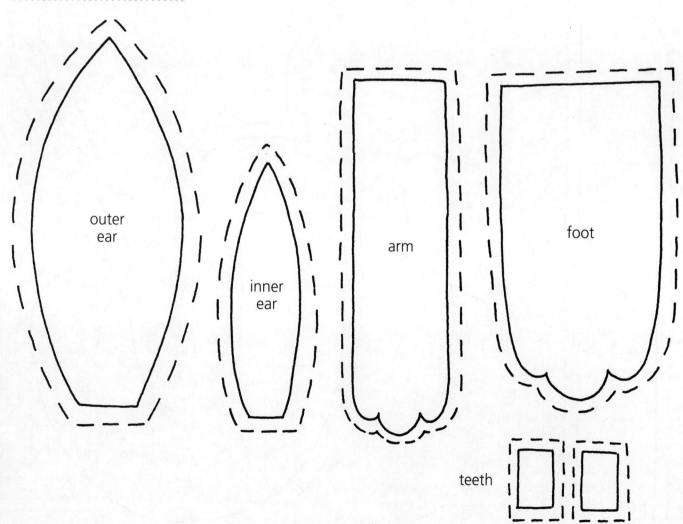

outer
ear

inner
ear

arm

foot

teeth

Umbrella Flower Patterns

umbrella

stem

leaf

handle

Follow-the-Directions Art Activities Scholastic Teaching Resources

How to Make
a Cute Caterpillar

Getting Started

Before introducing this activity, talk with students about the body parts of a caterpillar. Explain that caterpillars have segmented bodies made of flexible tissue that enables them to twist around. Caterpillars are equipped with large jaws for chewing leaves. Most caterpillars have eight pairs of legs. Three pairs on the front of the body are true legs. The remaining five pairs are small suction-like claspers for holding onto leaves. Invite students to come up with ways to move their fingers to show how a caterpillar moves and changes. For example, they may wiggle one finger to show the caterpillar crawling, open their hand wide to show it bursting through its skin, make a fist to represent a chrysalis, and flap their hands to show the butterfly flying away.

What You Need (for each child)

- Cute Caterpillar directions, pages 64–65
- cardboard egg cartons, cut into half, lengthwise
- tempera paint, assorted colors
- paintbrushes
- pipe cleaners, assorted colors, cut into 6-inch pieces
- pencil
- two wiggle eyes
- glue
- marker
- decorating materials (pom-poms, sequins, pieces of pipe cleaners, and so on)

Tips for Success

❋ Ahead of time, precut the egg cartons in half, lengthwise.

❋ Poke two holes in one end of the egg carton through which children will thread the pipe cleaner "feelers." Children may need some assistance inserting the pipe cleaner through the holes.

❋ To build vocabulary, tell children that another name for a caterpillar's feelers is *antennae*.

Do More!

Help children learn about the stages of metamorphosis, from caterpillar to butterfly. Set up a viewing station in your classroom. (Insect Lore Products—**www.insectlore.com**—is a good source for obtaining live larvae.) Invite children to observe the caterpillars as they build their chrysalides and develop into butterflies. Have students keep a journal of their observations. Once the caterpillars change into butterflies, have a butterfly release ceremony to say good-bye to your new friends.

How to Make a Cute Caterpillar

1st:  **Paint** the half egg carton.

Make a pattern, if you like.

Let the paint dry.

2nd:  **Add** feelers.

Poke the pipe cleaner

through the two holes

in the half egg carton.

3rd: **Use** a pencil to **curl** the ends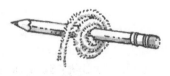

of the pipe cleaner.

Follow-the-Directions Art Activities   Scholastic Teaching Resources

4th: **Glue** two wiggle eyes

to the half egg carton.

Glue them below the feelers.

 **Draw** a smile.

 **Decorate** your caterpillar.

Use pipe cleaner pieces,

pom-poms, and more.

What a cute caterpillar!

Follow-the-Directions Art Activities   Scholastic Teaching Resources

 **How to Make**

a Beautiful Butterfly

Literature Links

Becoming Butterflies by Anne F. Rockwell (Walker and Co., 2002)
A teacher brings three monarch caterpillars into the classroom. Students follow the transformation from caterpillars into butterflies. Then the children wave good-bye as they let the butterflies go and watch them fly away.

The Butterfly Alphabet by Kjell B. Sandved (Scholastic, 1996)
This gorgeous book features spectacular close-up photos of butterfly wings, each revealing a pattern that resembles a letter in the alphabet.

Monarch Butterfly by Gail Gibbons (Holiday House, 1991)
A wonderful nonfiction book that teaches students about the life cycle, body parts, and behaviors of monarch butterflies.

Getting Started

As a warm-up to this project, review with students the concept of symmetry. Show students pictures of butterflies (see Literature Links, left). Ask them to study the wings. What do they notice about them? (*The wings are* symmetrical—*each side matches the other side exactly.*) Then have them practice creating symmetrical designs by giving them each a sheet of paper, folded in half, and then unfolded. Pair up students. On one side of the paper, one student creates a design using pattern blocks. The second student then duplicates the symmetrical design on the other half. Now students will be ready to create their own beautiful, symmetrical butterflies!

What You Need (for each child)

- Beautiful Butterfly directions, pages 67–68
- butterfly pattern, page 78
- pencil
- scissors
- tissue paper in light colors, 9 by 12 inches
- markers
- spring-type wooden clothespin
- black pipe cleaners, cut into 6-inch pieces

Tips for Success

❋ For very young children, you might precut the tissue paper butterflies, and omit the first step.

❋ To make the feelers more secure, students can dab a bit of glue on the bent pipe cleaner before clipping it inside the clothespin.

❋ You may substitute colorful plastic clothespins, if you like. However, in the seventh step, students will need to glue wiggle eyes onto their butterfly, instead of drawing a face.

❋ To turn the butterflies into magnets, attach magnetic tape to the back.

❋ For another activity that involves symmetry, see How to make a Valentine Mouse, page 36.

Do More!

Read to students an informational book about the stages of development of a butterfly (see Literature Links, left). Talk about what happens to the caterpillar in each stage. Then help children review the butterfly's life cycle with this fun activity. Divide the class into groups. Have students fold a sheet of construction paper into quarters, and then reopen it. Next, give each group a paper plate on which you've placed a few grains of rice (to represent eggs), tube-shaped pasta (caterpillars), scraps of green construction paper (leaves), shell macaroni (chrysalides), and bow-shaped pasta (butterflies). Also provide markers and glue. Invite children to use the materials to recreate a butterfly's life cycle. Encourage children to number each stage.

How to Make
a Beautiful Butterfly

1st:  **Trace** and **cut** out

 the butterfly.

Use tissue paper.

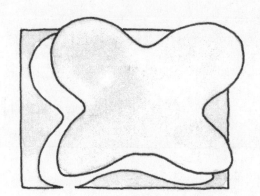

2nd: **Fold** your butterfly

$\frac{1}{2}$ in half. **Use** markers

to **draw** designs

1 $\frac{1}{2}$ on one half.

3rd: **Unfold** your butterfly.

Now both sides match!

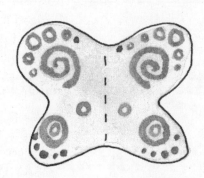

Follow-the-Directions Art Activities Scholastic Teaching Resources

Cut off this bottom strip along the dotted line. Then glue this page to the top of page 68.

67

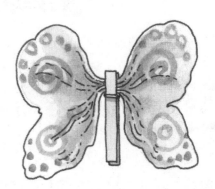

4th:  **Gather** the butterfly

in the middle.

Clip it inside the clothespin.

5th:  **Add** feelers.

$\frac{1}{2}$

Bend the pipe cleaner in half.

Clip it inside the clothespin.

6th:  **Use** a pencil to **curl**

the ends of the pipe cleaner.

7th:  **Draw** a face.

Fly away, butterfly!

Follow-the-Directions Art Activities Scholastic Teaching Resources

 **How to Make**

an American Flag

Getting Started

Look at the American flag with your class. Ask them why they think the flag is often referred to as the "Stars and Stripes." Invite them to point out and count these features. Then explain that the 13 stripes stand for each of America's original thirteen colonies. The 50 stars stand for each state in our country today. The flag is a symbol of freedom and pride in our nation. You might also show children examples of how the flag looked during past periods in our country's history (see Literature Links, right). Invite them to discuss the similarities and differences between the flags. Then tell children that they are each going to make an American flag.

What You Need (for each child)

• American Flag directions, pages 70–71
• stars rectangle, page 79
• scissors
• six white construction paper strips, $1/2$ by 12 inches
• seven red construction paper strips, $1/2$ by 12 inches
• white paper, $6^1/2$ by 12 inches
• glue
• blue marker
• two plastic drinking straws
• tape

Tips for Success

❋ Make a photocopy (not a tracer pattern) of the stars rectangle for each child.

❋ Highlight the color words in the directions using markers in corresponding colors.

❋ In the third step, students should line up the strips close together on the large white paper rectangle to cover it. You might suggest that they practice placing the strips side by side in an ABAB pattern before they apply glue.

❋ To make the long straw needed in the sixth step, insert the end of one straw inside the other. This will create a "flagpole" to which students can tape their flag.

Do More!

Invite students to design their own flags that tell about themselves—their interests, likes, dislikes, families, pets, and so on. Display the flags and ask children to try guessing which flag each student designed.

Literature Links

The Flag We Love by Pam Munoz Ryan (Charlesbridge, 1996) Through easy-to-read rhyming verse and vivid illustrations, this book depicts the flag's importance throughout our nation's history.

Red, White and Blue: The Story of the American Flag by John Herman (Grosset & Dunlop, 1998) This book explores, in simple terms, the history of our nation's flag and how it has changed over the years.

The Pledge of Allegiance (Scholastic, 2000) Available in two versions, English and bilingual, this book includes gorgeous color photos that illustrate words and phrases in our country's pledge.

1st:  **Count** six strips

of white paper.

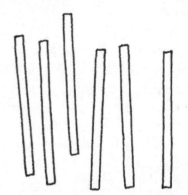

2nd: **Count** seven strips

of red paper.

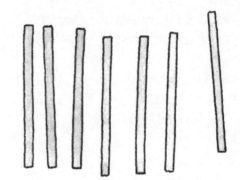

3rd: **Glue** the strips to the

large white rectangle

in an ABAB pattern.

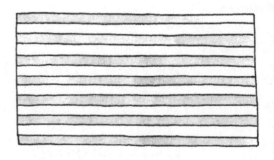

Start with a red strip.

70

Cut off this bottom strip along the dotted line. Then glue this page to the top of page 71.

Follow-the-Directions Art Activities Scholastic Teaching Resources

 **4th:** **Use** a blue marker to **color**

the background

of the small rectangle with the stars.

 **5th:** **Glue** the rectangle

to the top left corner

of your flag.

 **6th:** **Tape** the long straw

to the back of your flag

on the left.

Now wave your flag!

How to Make
a Paper Plate Crab

Getting Started

Before students make their paper plate crabs, invite them to learn about this fascinating creature's body parts. They may be interested to find out that a crab's two front claws (or *pincers*, used for feeding and defense), are actually legs. In addition, crabs have four more pairs of jointed legs that help them walk sideways on land and swim in the ocean. (Students may enjoy adding these additional legs, cut from paper, to their paper plate crabs.)

What You Need (for each child)

- Paper Plate Crab directions, pages 73–74
- claw pattern, page 79
- large paper plate, cut in half
- tempera paints, assorted colors
- paintbrush
- pencil
- scissors
- construction paper, assorted colors, 7 by 8 inches
- glue
- pipe cleaner
- two wiggle eyes
- red marker

Tips for Success

❋ Precut the paper plates and let students paint the back (convex side) of the half plates ahead of time. Or, you may opt to have students cut the plates in half and paint them as part of the activity. Use the pictures and labels on page 81 to include these additional steps.

❋ In the second and fourth steps, students should attach the claws and the bent pipe cleaner to the unpainted front side of the half plate (the concave side).

❋ As an alternative to gluing the claws and the pipe cleaner to the front of the half plate, students may staple these parts in place.

❋ In the fourth step, instead of using wiggle eyes, children can make their own crab eyes using scrap paper and scissors.

Do More!

Talk with students about the types of environments in which crabs live. (Many crabs live in the ocean but there are some varieties that live on land, near the shore.) As a group, make a list of other creatures that live in the same habitat. Examples might include starfish, sea urchins, barnacles, mussels, sea anemones, and snails. If your students do not live near the beach or ocean or have never visited one, share informational books about this topic (see Literature Links, left) to provide them with some background knowledge about beach environments. Then challenge students to come up with ways to create some of these other creatures using arts and craft materials.

How to Make
a Paper Plate Crab

  2

1st: **Trace** and **cut** out two claws.

Use colored paper.

2nd: **Glue** the claws to the unpainted side

of the half plate as shown.

$\frac{1}{2}$

3rd: **Bend** the pipe cleaner in half.

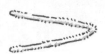

4th: **Glue** wiggle eyes to the ends

of the bent pipe cleaner.

Let the glue dry.

Cut off this bottom strip along the dotted line. Then glue this page to the top of page 74.

73

Glue this page to the bottom of page 73.

 **5th:** **Glue** the bent pipe cleaner

to the unpainted side

of the half plate as shown.

Let the glue dry.

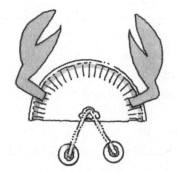

 **6th:** **Turn** the half plate over

to the painted side.

Bend the pipe cleaner

pieces so they stand up.

 **7th:** **Draw** a smile on your crab.

Clap your claws!

74

Follow-the-Directions Art Activities Scholastic Teaching Resources

 How to Make

a Sunny Visor

Getting Started

Introduce this activity by playing Guess What's in the Box—a fun
game that will also sharpen children's critical thinking skills. Put a
sun visor in a box or a bag so that your students cannot see it. Tell
them that in your box is an item of clothing that can be worn in the
summer. Invite them to ask questions about the visor that require
only a response of "yes" or "no." As students continue to ask
questions, write on a chart the information children's questions have
revealed. How many questions will it take until someone guesses
what's inside?

What You Need (for each child)

- Sun Visor directions, pages 76–77
- visor and sun patterns, page 80
- large paper plate
- scissors
- pencil
- construction paper, assorted colors, 6 by 10 inches
- yellow construction paper, 5 by 5 inches
- glue
- decorating materials (scrap paper, crayons, stickers, and so on)

Tips for Success

❋ In the fourth step, have students glue the visor to the convex side
of the paper plate rim.

❋ In the fifth step, highlight the word *yellow* with a yellow marker.

❋ If the paper plate rim is too small to fit on a student's head,
simply trim away more of the plate.

❋ Use craft foam instead of construction paper to make the visors,
if desired.

Do More!

Discuss sun safety with students. Besides wearing their visors, talk
about other ways that children can protect themselves from the
sun. (*stay in the shade, use sunblock, wear protective clothing* and
sunglasses, never look directly at the sun, and so on) Invite students
to share the information they learned by creating sun safety posters
to display in your school.

Literature Links

Cool Ali by Nancy Poydar
(Margaret K. McElderry
Books, 1996)
How do you keep cool
on a hot summer day in
the city? Ali finds a way
by using her imagination,
colored chalk, and the
sidewalk!

*Summer: An Alphabet
Acrostic* by Steven Schnur
(Clarion, 2001)
Celebrate summer from
A to Z with this clever
collection of acrostic
poems illustrated in
vibrant colors.

a Make a Sunny Visor

1st: **Fold** a paper plate in half.

2nd: **Cut** out the inside

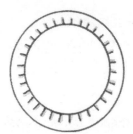

of the plate, leaving the rim.

Unfold the rim.

3rd: **Trace** and **cut** out

a visor. **Use** colored paper.

 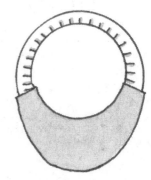

4th: **Glue** the edge of the visor

to the rim of the plate.

Let the glue dry.

Follow-the-Directions Art Activities Scholastic Teaching Resources

5th: **Trace** and **cut** out a sun.

 **Use** yellow paper.

6th: **Glue** the sun

 to the visor.

Let the glue dry.

7th: **Decorate** your visor

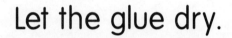 with scrap paper,

 crayons, and more.

8th: **Bend** the sun so it stands up.

 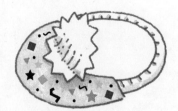

Have fun in the sun!

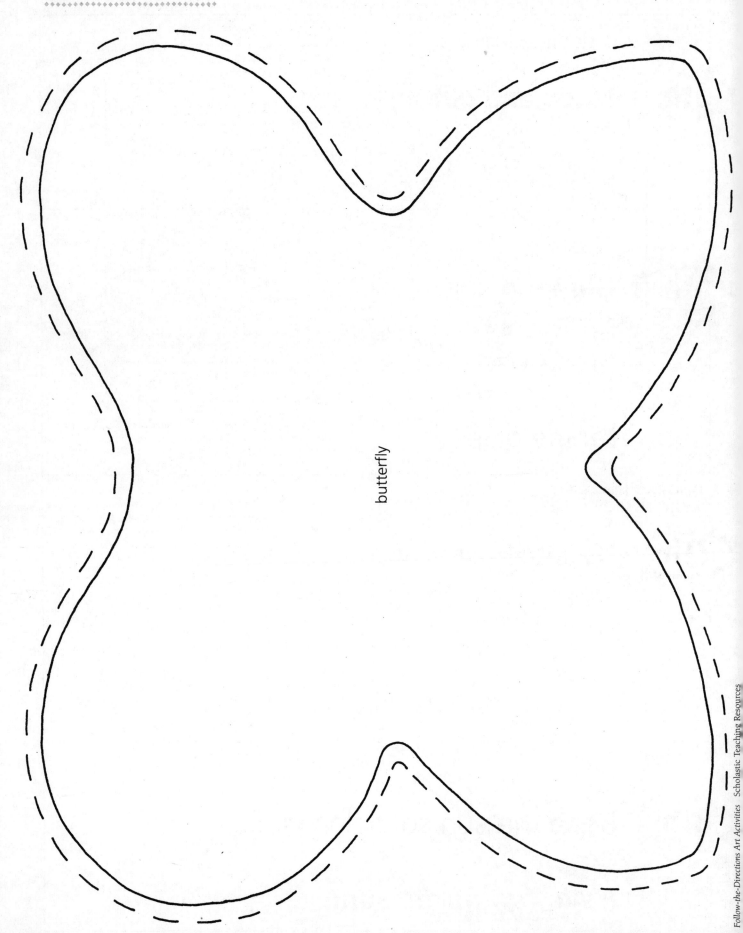

butterfly

American Flag Pattern

stars rectangle

Paper Plate Crab Pattern

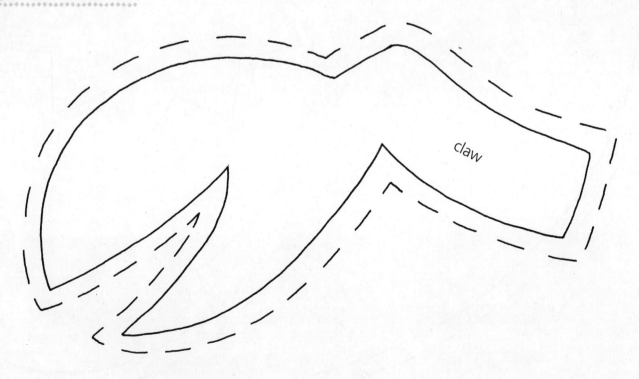

claw

visor

sun

Follow-the-Directions Art Activities Scholastic Teaching Resources